The Birthday Card

Story by Viki Bennett

and Nicki O'Brien

Illustrated by Judy Brown

SALE
£25.99

50%
OFF!

POST OFFICE
ENTRANCE
SECOND CLASS
FIRST CLASS
NO DOGS
OPENING TIMES
9am - 5.30pm

CARD SHOP
GIFT BOXES
PARTY BALLOONS PARTY BAGS AND MUCH MORE
OPEN
IT'S A BOY
HUG ME IT'S MY BIRTHDAY

TRAVEL INSURANCE
NATIONAL SAVINGS

60
60
21
HAPPY BIRTHDAY
CONGRATULATIONS
NEW BABY
NEW BABY GIRL
ITS A BOY
HAPPY BIRTHDAY
ON YOUR 3rd BIRTHDAY
On your 5th Birthday
To a special 6 year old
To a cute 6 year old
You Are 3
HOORAY
Happy
5 today!
HAPPY BIRTHDAY 6

1st
2nd
POST
OFFICE
PENS

NINA

SALE
£25.99
It's your birthday
5

50%
OFF
It's
thday
5

It's your birthday
5
5
Josh